Adaptation and Survival

Robert Snedden

Chicago, Illinois

www.capstonepub.com
Visit our website to find out more information about Heinemann-Raintree books.

To order:
☎ Phone 888-454-2279
🖱 Visit www.capstonepub.com to browse our catalog and order online.

© 2012 Raintree
an imprint of Capstone Global Library, LLC
Chicago, Illinois

All rights reserved. No part of this publication may be reproduced or transmitted in any form or by any means, electronic or mechanical, including photocopying, recording, taping, or any information storage and retrieval system, without permission in writing from the publisher.

Edited by Andrew Farrow, Adrian Vigliano, and Diyan Leake
Designed by Victoria Allen
Picture research by Elizabeth Alexander
Illustrations by Oxford Designers & Illustrators

Originated by Capstone Global Library Ltd
Printed and bound in the United States by Corporate Graphics

15 14 13 12 11
10 9 8 7 6 5 4 3 2 1

Library of Congress Cataloging-in-Publication Data
Cataloging-in-Publication data is on file at the Library of Congress.

ISBN: 978-1-4109-4428-3 (HC) 978-1-4109-4435-1 (PB)

Acknowledgments
The author and publisher are grateful to the following for permission to reproduce copyright material: Alamy p. 35 (© GoSeeFoto); Dreamstime.com pp. 7 (© Nico Smit), 8 (© Outdoorsman), 22 (© Robert Venn); FLPA p. 23 (Mark Moffett/Minden Pictures); Getty Images p. 13 (Annie Griffiths Belt); iStockphoto pp. 29 (© MaXPdia), 38 (© ihoe); Nature Picture Library p. 26 (© Bence Mate); NHPA p. 40 (Dave Watts); Photolibrary pp. 9 (M. Varesvuo), 10 (Wayne Lynch), 11 (Doug Allan), 12 (Naftali Hilger), 14 (Arthur V. Evans), 19 (M. Varesvuo), 20 (Kerstin Hinze), 21 (Alain Dragesco-Joffé), 25 (Fritz Poelking), 24 (François Gilson), 27 (Gerard Lacz), 30 (Richard Herrmann), 32 (Tim Zurowski), 41 (James Gerholdt); Shutterstock pp. 4 (© Gentoo Multimedia Ltd), 5 (© worldswildlifewonders), 6 (© Rido), 15 (© Zolran), 18 (© Maynard Case), 31 (© Studio 37), 33 (© Bobkeenan Photography), 36 (© Jon Naustdalslid), 39 (© Arto Hakola).

Cover photograph of common bottlenose dolphins (*Tursiops truncatus*) reproduced with permission of FLPA (© Jurgen & Christine Sohns).

Every effort has been made to contact copyright holders of material reproduced in this book. Any omissions will be rectified in subsequent printings if notice is given to the publisher.

Contents

Some words appear in the text in bold, **like this**. You can find out what they mean by looking in the glossary.

Survival of the Fittest

Our planet, Earth, has many different **environments**. Environments are places where living things are found. These range from regions full of ice to hot, dry deserts. Each environment presents challenges to the living things there.

Adaptations

Living things must develop features that help them survive in their environments. These features are called **adaptations**. The stripes of a tiger are an adaptation. Stripes help a tiger blend into its surroundings while it hunts for food. A tiger that catches enough food is more likely to survive than a tiger without this adaptation.

The emperor penguin (below) and quetzel (at right) have adaptations that help them survive in very different environments.

Fit for life

Scientists talk about the "**fitness**" of living things. The fittest living things are the ones that fit best into their environment. They develop the best adaptations.

Only the fittest living things will survive. They will produce young that survive, too. These plants and animals, such as the striped tiger, will become the strongest and most common of their kind. This process is called **natural selection**.

Temperature Control

Living things rely on thousands of processes, or actions, that keep them alive. For example, they must break down food **to** get **energy** (the ability to do work). These processes must take place at certain temperatures. If the temperature is not right, these processes begin to fail.

Animals have a number of **adaptations** to keep them at the right temperature. Sometimes these are body responses, such as sweating. Sometimes they are **behaviors** (the way a living thing acts), such as looking for shade.

WHAT IT MEANS FOR US

Some scientists think that humans developed naked skin to survive hot conditions. This was an adaptation. But our heads stayed hairy. This is because the hair protects the brain from direct sunshine.

Inside and out

Mammals are warm-blooded animals with backbones and hair, like humans. Mammals and birds are able to create energy from the food they eat. This energy is in the form of heat. Their blood carries heat around the body. This and other body processes, such as sweating, help to keep body temperatures at the right level. Behaviors such as finding shade also help.

Reptiles are cold-blooded animals. They are often covered with scales, like lizards. A reptile's body temperature increases if its surroundings are hot. Its body temperature falls if its surroundings are cold. It has body processes that keep its temperature at the right level (see box below right).Reptiles also have behaviors that affect their body temperature. For example, they lie in the Sun to get warm.

Color correction

Some lizards can adjust their body temperature by changing color. In the morning, their skin darkens. This is because dark colors are better at taking in heat. As the day warms up, their skin lightens. The lighter color reflects, or pushes away, some of the Sun's rays. This prevents the lizard from getting too hot.

Keeping warm

Earth has many cold places, such as high mountains. One of the biggest challenges for living things in these places is staying warm. One way to do this is by using **insulation**. Insulation is a layer that holds in heat.

Mammals such as the Arctic fox have a thick layer of fuzzy under-fur that holds in heat. Over this is a second layer of longer and thicker hairs. These hairs keep the under-fur dry. Birds have a layer of fluffy feathers, called down, next to their skin. This works just like a mammal's under-fur. It holds in heat.

The thick fur of the Arctic fox protects it from the cold.

Cold-climate trees

Conifers are trees with cones (like pinecones) and needle-like leaves. Pine trees are an example of conifers. Conifers and other trees have **adaptations** to deal with cold weather. During winter in cold **environments**, most of the water in the ground will be frozen. Conifers' needle-like leaves help them. These leaves are covered with a waxy coating. This coating prevents water loss. This adaptation means that the leaves have water even during frozen winters.

Conifer trees' cone-shape is another important adaptation. This shape allows heavy snow to fall more easily from their branches, leaving them undamaged.

Chilly legs

Most birds have bare legs. But the Arctic ptarmigan (left) and the snowy owl are different. They are among the few birds that have feathers on their legs and feet. This helps them survive in cold places.

Warm in the water

Many animals spend all or part of their lives in the water. Yet temperatures in the coldest parts of the oceans can be near freezing. How do animals survive there?

All **mammals** have a layer of fat underneath their skin. This reduces the loss of heat to the animal's surroundings. Whales, seals, and other mammals that live in water have a thicker layer of fat than mammals that live on land. This extra-thick fat is called **blubber**.

A group of Pacific walruses turn pink as they lose extra heat.

Overheating

But animals with blubber can get too hot when they leave the water. Just as humans do, walruses turn pink when they are hot. This is because the flow of blood increases near the surface of the skin. This allows extra heat to escape.

Natural antifreeze

In chilly waters, temperatures can be lower than the freezing point of fish blood. To survive, some fish produce something called **glycoproteins** in their blood. These stop ice crystals from forming in their bodies.

WHAT IT MEANS FOR US

We use a substance called **antifreeze** in cars. Water helps some parts of the car work. Antifreeze stops this water from freezing in cold weather. Antifreeze works the same way as the glycoproteins in the blood of cold-water fish.

Cold-water fish like this Antarctic ice fish have a natural kind of antifreeze in their blood. This helps them survive in freezing waters.

WORD BANK
blubber   layer of fat found under the skin of mammals that live in water, such as whales
antifreeze   substance added to water to prevent it from freezing

The Camel

Animals in hot deserts face high daytime temperatures. They also have little water. The camel has **adapted** to survive in these challenging conditions.

Water conservation

Camels in the desert need to make good use of any water they find. For this reason, losing heat by sweating would not be a good **adaptation** to desert life. Cooling down this way would mean losing precious water.

Water loss

Camels do all they can to save water. Still, they can lose up to 30 percent of their body's water and survive. (Most animals die if they lose 15 percent of their body's water.) When water becomes available, a camel can drink 20 percent of its body weight in 10 minutes!

Heat storage

Instead, camels store heat in their bodies. A camel's body temperature can rise slightly over the course of the day. At night, when conditions are much cooler, the heat stored by the camel is released into the air. The camel's body temperature then returns to its normal level. No water is lost through sweating.

Common confusions

The camel's hump

Camels do not store water in their humps. The hump is made mostly of fat. It is used as a food supply.

The jack rabbit has a different way to keep cool. Its large ears help it cool down. They give off heat. They keep the rabbit from getting too hot.

Hibernation

Animals can have trouble finding food during the winter. Some animals, especially birds, avoid this by **migrating**. They move to warmer places when the cold weather comes. Others escape winter by **hibernating**. They rest in a way that requires little **energy.**

Extreme survival

Young red flat bark beetles survive through the cold winter in the state of Alaska. As winter approaches, these insects produce something in their blood that acts like **antifreeze**. They also begin to lose water from their bodies. All of this helps them survive.

Preparing for winter

Before hibernating, some animals build up a supply of fat in their bodies. This will provide them with enough energy to get through winter. They may dig a tunnel or find a hollow tree or a cave. This is where they will rest.

Adult red flat bark beetles are found under the bark of logs.

Insulating materials

The fur of a hibernating **mammal** acts as **insulation** against the winter chill. The animal will also find materials such as twigs, leaves, and feathers to build a nest. This offers extra protection.

Into hibernation

As it hibernates, the animal's body systems, such as its heart beat, slow down. The animal is using much less energy than it would normally need to stay alive.

Common confusions

"Hibernating" bears

Bears do not truly hibernate. In their winter dens, their temperature drops just a few degrees below its normal level. They do become very sleepy. But they can quickly become fully awake again if disturbed.

A hibernating bat uses 99 percent less energy than it uses when fully active.

WORD BANK
migrate   move from one area to another every year or season
hibernate   sleep deeply during the winter months to save energy

The Arctic Ground Squirrel

The Arctic ground squirrel lives in the forests and grassy areas of very cold places like northern Canada. The ground squirrel survives cold winter temperatures by **hibernating**.

The squirrel's year

The Arctic ground squirrel has a long, round body. It has stubby legs and sharp claws. These are all **adaptations** to a life spent partly underground. Their homes are made up of several underground **burrows**, or tunnels.

The squirrels are active from around the end of April until early October. The adult males are usually the first to come out from hibernating. The females give birth to 5 to 10 pups in June. The young develop quickly. By late summer they will have left the burrows where they were born. Adult squirrels are ready to hibernate by late August. The young squirrels take longer to build up enough fat. They may be active until late September.

Shaking and shivering

Every two or three weeks, the squirrel begins to shake and shiver. It will do this for 12 to 15 hours. This warms it back up to a normal body temperature. After it stops shivering, its temperature begins to fall below zero again. Scientists are not sure why the squirrel does this.

Cool squirrels

The ground squirrel will spend between seven and eight months hibernating. While hibernating, the squirrel's body temperature falls to the lowest ever measured in a **mammal**. It falls a few degrees below freezing.

The ground squirrel eats to gain weight.
It also stores extra food and lines its
burrow with grass and hair.

The baby ground squirrels
leave the burrow
in mid-summer.

The ground squirrel's body
temperature falls as it becomes
less active. Hibernation begins.

Females have
their young less
than one month
after mating.

Deep
hibernation.

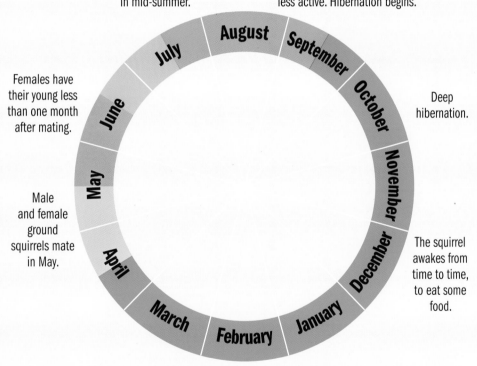

August
July
September
October
June
November
May
December
April
January
March
February

Male
and female
ground
squirrels mate
in May.

The squirrel
awakes from
time to time,
to eat some
food.

The ground squirrels awake fully in the spring.

Defense and Attack

All animals need to find food. They eat plants, other animals, or both plants and animals. In order to survive, plants and animals must avoid being eaten.

To survive, living things develop **adaptations**, such as:

- having thorns or poisonous leaves. This protects plants from being eaten.
- being part of a herd, or group, like zebras.
- being able to run swiftly, like an antelope.
- being big and powerful, like a water buffalo.

A large African water buffalo is big enough to scare off most predators.

Predator and prey

Predators are animals that catch and kill other animals. **Prey** are animals that are caught and eaten. A successful predator is **adapted** to catch and kill its prey. Meanwhile, its prey must be adapted to survive the attacks of its predator. The two animals **evolve** (change over time) in response to each other.

Bats versus moths

Bats make high clicking sounds as they hunt moths. They use the echoes of these sounds to find moths in the dark (see page 37).

Some moths change their path when they hear the bats' clicks. They also make clicks of their own, to confuse the bat. But some bats use clicks that are beyond what moths can hear. Some even make their clicks quieter as they get closer to their prey.

Smaller birds can work together to drive off a larger predator. This **behavior** is called mobbing.

Camouflage

Many animals are protected by **camouflage**. This means that they have colorings and markings that help them to blend into the background. They can avoid being noticed by **predators**—or by **prey**.

Where's that bug?

Some caterpillars use camouflage to look like twigs. Stick insects look just like sticks. Moths use camouflage to avoid being spotted by passing birds. This is a very important **adaptation** for an insect that is active at night, but rests during the day.

Can you spot the lappet moth clinging to the branch in this photograph? It looks just like a leaf.

Sitting tight

Female birds usually look after eggs in the nest. Bright colors would draw the attention of a predator. So, female birds are often drab colors like brown and gray. They use camouflage to blend in with the nest.

Mimicry

Others animals **mimic** other animals, meaning they act or look like them. For example, the king snake is harmless. But it has markings that are very similar to those of the **venomous** (poisonous) coral snake. A predator cannot tell the difference. So, to be safe, it leaves the king snake alone.

The ground-nesting Egyptian nightjar is well camouflaged by its brown feathers.

WORD BANK
camouflage   colorings or markings that help an animal blend into the background
mimic   act or look like another animal

Plant defenses

Plants produce a variety of defenses.

Sharp deterrents

Thorns, spines, and prickles are common plant defenses. All three **adaptations** do a similar job. They scare off **predators**, such as insects, with the threat of getting hurt.

Invisible weapons

Many plants use invisible weapons to protect themselves. For instance, the fine hairs on the leaves of the stinging nettle contain a substance that can harm the skin. Some plants release substances that affect an insect's body, making it starve to death. Others **mimic** scents (smells) insects use to warn of danger. These scents make the insects move away, thinking there is a predator nearby.

The foxglove produces poisonous substances that make insects avoid it. It is dangerous for humans, too.

Working together

Some plants attract their own private army of protectors. The macaranga tree grows in the forests of Asia, Africa, and Australia. Its hollow stems make good nesting places for ants. The tree also provides food for the ants. In return, the ants protect the tree. They fight off other plant-eating insects.

The partnership between these ants and the tree is good for both of them.

Catching and killing

Predators have developed features that allow them to catch and kill their **prey**.

The teeth of a tiger deliver a killing bite to its prey.

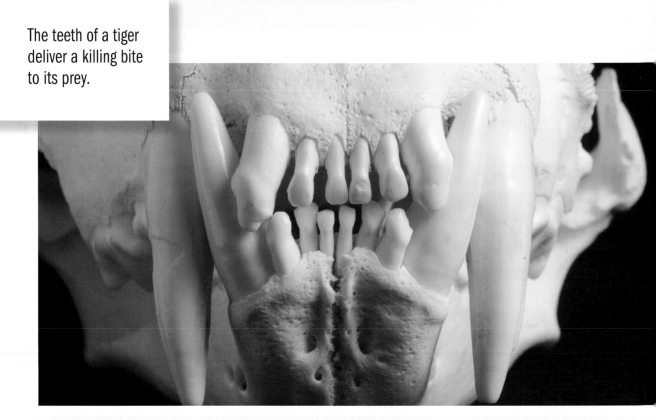

Swift killers

Cheetahs have many **adaptations** that make them the fastest hunters on land. They have flexible **spines** (the series of bones up and down the back). They also have flexible **joints** (connections between bones that allow movement). They have powerful leg muscles and large lungs. Prey cannot usually cannot outrun cheetahs' quick attack.

Air-to-water hunter

The osprey is a large **bird of prey**. It hunts and kills other animals. The osprey has many adaptations that help it catch fish. It soars high above the water, searching out its prey with its good eyesight. After plunging in the water. It pushes its sharp **talons** (claws) forward to grab the fish. Short spikes on the underside of its toes help the osprey grip its slippery catch.

The osprey is **adapted** for scooping fish from the water.

On the tip of its tongue

A frog's tongue is attached to the front of its mouth. It lies folded over inside. If the frog sees food, it flips its tongue out. A sticky tip on the tongue captures the prey. It then pulls the prey back into the frog's mouth. These are all adaptations.

On the Move

Animals have many amazing ways to get from one place to another. These include walking, jumping, swimming, flying, and crawling.

Life without legs

Snakes have become **adapted** to a life without legs. Their bodies can move almost silently over the ground as they hunt for **prey**.

Most snakes move by using a winding movement. The tail pushes against the ground and moves the snake forward. Some snakes pull up their tails and bunch themselves up like coiled springs. They then thrust their heads forward as they straighten out their bodies. Big snakes grip the ground with special belly scales. They pull their bodies along like a caterpillar.

The basilisk lizard can escape danger by running quickly across the surface of the water. Its feet work like paddles. They keep it from sinking.

Through the trees

Many **mammals** are at home in trees. The sharp claws and flexible legs of squirrels are **adaptations** for running up and down trees. Apes, such as gibbons, have arms adapted to tree life. They swing effortlessly through the treetops on their long arms. They also use their arms to balance as they run over the branches.

A gibbon swings through the trees.

Walking, running, and jumping

Many animals, such as mice and humans, walk on the flats of their feet. This **adaptation** makes them steady on their feet. Other animals move on tiptoe. This adaptation increases the length of their steps. It means more **joints** are used in moving the leg forward. This makes an animal faster.

Ready to run

Mammals adapted for running move on what we would think of as their fingers and toes. Dogs' and cats' wrists and heels never touch the ground as they move along. Thick pads behind the animals' claws give them extra grip and protection.

Hoofed animals, such as deer, only have two toes on the ground. What appears to be a horse's foot is just a single toe. Its hoof is an adapted toenail.

Mammals have different ways of standing. It depends on how the bones of their feet touch the ground. Each has its advantages. Humans are steady on their feet. Dogs have both speed and power. Deer have speed.

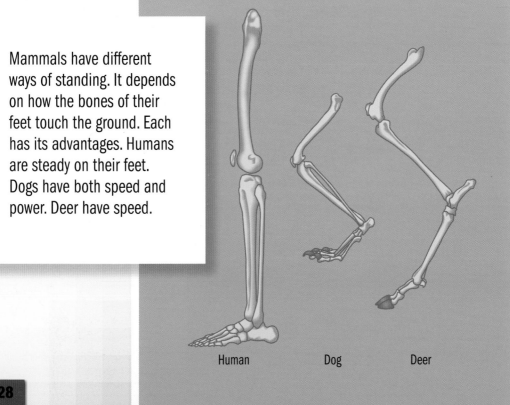

Human   Dog   Deer

Kangaroo hop

Some animals jump rather than walk or run. The kangaroo has large **tendons** in its hind legs. Tendons are rough bands that connect muscle to bone. These tendons store **energy** and push the kangaroo forward. This is instead of using muscle power alone. The kangaroo's large tail helps it to stay balanced as it jumps. These adaptations allow the kangaroo to use little energy as it travels large distances in search of food.

Floating, jet propulsion, and streamlining

Many living things are **adapted** to move through the water. Some animals, such as jellyfish, mostly float along with the moving ocean. They use no **energy** to get from one place to another. But they have little choice about where they go.

Octopuses and squid can move by **jet propulsion.** This means they suck in water and then blast it back out again. This uses a lot of energy. But it can provide a sudden burst of speed to escape danger or catch **prey**. Most of the time these animals use their fins (or arms, in the case of octopuses) to move around.

Most fish have **streamlined** bodies. This means their shape lets water pass by easily. This **adaptation** allows them to move quickly. It also saves energy as they move.

The streamlined body of the blue finned tuna allows it to move swiftly through the water.

fins

Swim bladder

Most fish have a sort of air-filled bag inside them called a **swim bladder**. By adjusting the amount of air in the swim bladder, the fish can move up and down in the water. More air in the swim bladder makes the fish rise. Less air makes it sink.

Dolphins leap from the water. This type of movement uses less energy than swimming through the water.

WORD BANK
jet propulsion movement created by sucking in water and then blasting it out again
streamlined having a design that lets air or water pass by easily

Insect air force

Most kinds of insect can fly. Many insects, such as flies, don't flap their wings directly. Rather, their wings are attached to the middle section of the insect. Powerful muscles inside the insect's body change its shape very rapidly. This movement causes the attached wings to go up and down. These **adaptations** allow for very rapid wing beats. Insects such as dragonflies use muscles to move their wings directly. One set of muscles pulls the wings down. Another set raises them again.

Built to fly

Most birds have adaptations that allow them to fly. Instead of front legs, birds have wings. They have powerful breast muscles. They use these muscles to launch themselves upward. They also have lightweight bones (see box on page 33). Weighing less means they need to use less **energy** to fly.

Dragonflies are very fast and talented fliers.

Seed dispersal

Plants make use of wind to get from one place to another. The seeds of plants such as orchids are so tiny that they can be blown long distances. Maple and sycamore trees have seeds with wing shapes. These spin through the air as they fall, landing far away from the parent tree. That way, the seedlings will not compete with the parent tree for light and water.

Light as a feather

To keep their weight down, birds have light, hollow bones. All the bones of some birds can actually weigh less than their feathers.

The wing-like shape of the sycamore seed makes it spin through the air.

Senses

Seeing

The sense of sight is a powerful **adaptation**. Good vision helps animals spot danger (or a possible meal) from far away.

An animal's **field of vision** is what it can see without moving its head. The eyes of **prey** animals are often placed far back on the sides of their heads. This adaptation gives them a good all-around field of vision. The eyes of **predators** are more likely to be placed at the front of their heads. This adaptation allows them to judge distances. That way, they know how far away their prey is.

Prey animals, such as a duck, generally have eyes on the sides and top of the head. This allows them to spot attacks from above, to the side, and behind. Predator animals, such as an owl, have forward-facing eyes. They see best in the downward and forward direction. This is an adaptation for hunting.

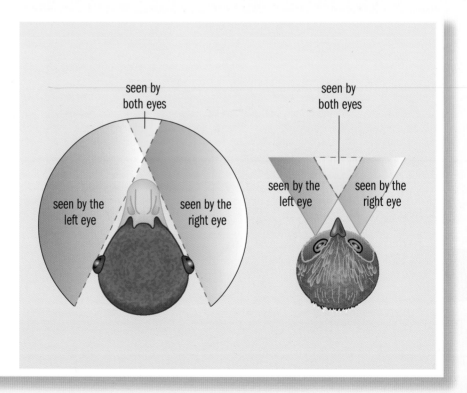

seen by both eyes

seen by both eyes

seen by the left eye

seen by the right eye

seen by the left eye

seen by the right eye

Seeing underwater

The **lens** is the part of the eye that **focuses** light. It adjusts to the light and lets the animal see clearly. The lens of a fish eye is almost perfectly round. Because of the way light travels underwater, a round lens makes it easy for fish to focus and see underwater. In contrast, humans' oval-shaped lenses do not focus well underwater. In this way, fish are **adapted** to see underwater—and to survive there.

Best of both worlds

A fish called anableps is found in the rivers of South and Central America. The anableps' eyes are adapted to see both in and out of the water. They can even do both at the same time. The fish can cruise just under the surface of the water. It watches for insects to eat above the surface. At the same time, it can look for danger from below.

The anableps has eyes that are divided in two. The top half can see in air. The bottom half can see underwater.

WORD BANK
field of vision everything that can be seen at the same time without turning the head or moving the eyes
lens part of the eye that focuses light

Hearing

Being able to hear is an important **adaptation**. Animals may hear approaching danger before it can be seen, such as the sound of a **predator** in the grass.

Antelope listen for the sound of an approaching predator.

Hearing ranges

Not all animals hear the same sounds. For example, dogs can hear sounds that are too high for us to hear. Snakes can **detect** (notice) very low sounds traveling through the ground in their bellies. Elephants also make use of low sounds to communicate.

Echolocation

When a bat flies, it produces sounds that are much too high for us to hear. These sounds echo back from objects around the bat. The bat detects these sounds with its special ears. The "sound picture" that a bat builds up allows it to hunt insects on a dark night. This process is called **echolocation**.

In echolocation, sound waves are sent out—for example, by a bat. The sound waves bounce off objects. These sound waves can then be picked up by the ears of a bat or dolphin. The sonar on board a submarine can also pick up sound waves.

WHAT IT MEANS FOR US

Humans make use of echolocation to keep track of objects. **Sonar** is an instrument that uses **sound waves** (traveling sound **energy**) to find objects underwater. Sonar sends out sound waves and listens for echoes. Fishing boats use sonar to find large groups of fish. Submarines use sonar to locate large objects that could get in their way.

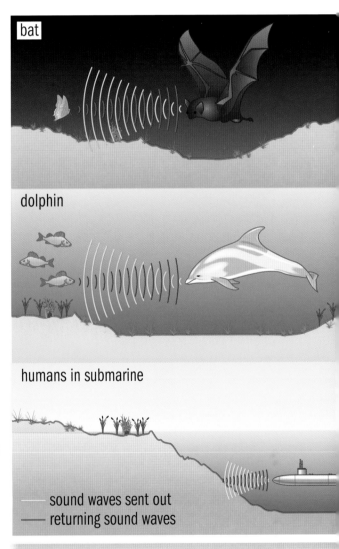

bat

dolphin

humans in submarine

— sound waves sent out
— returning sound waves

WORD BANK
echolocation   ability to detect something, based on the time it takes an echo to bounce back from it
sonar   instrument that uses sound waves to detect objects underwater

Smell and taste

A sense of smell is more important for some animals than others. Some fish have a very good sense of smell. Up to two-thirds of a shark's brain may be involved in sensing smells. This **adaptation** allows a shark to **detect** a single drop of blood in a swimming pool.

When salmon become adults, they leave the rivers where they began life to visit the ocean. When the time comes to lay their eggs, they find their way back to their home rivers. Scientists believe that they remember the smell and taste of home.

Salmon use their incredible sense of smell to guide them upriver to where they first hatched. They will even leap up waterfalls to get back home.

Bear necessities

Bears have perhaps the most sensitive sense of smell of all animals. They use it to find threats, mates, and meals. Bears have been known to detect the scent of a human up to 14 hours after the person has walked along a trail.

A brown bear stands tall to sniff the air.

Common confusions

Tasting or smelling?

Many **reptiles** don't use their tongues for tasting like we do. Snakes and lizards constantly flick their tongue in and out of their mouth. The tongue picks up tiny bits from the air. It carries these bits back into the reptile's mouth. It places them onto the reptile's scent **detectors**. Some people say a reptile smells something in the air. Others say it tastes something in the air.

WORD BANK
detect notice or pick up on
detector device that picks up on the presence of something, such as a sound or smell

Sixth senses

The picture that other animals build up of the world may be quite different from the one we have. Some animals use senses that we do not have at all.

Water sense

Fish have a line running along each side of their bodies. This is called the **lateral line**. Along this line there are rows of very sensitive **detectors**. These pick up changes in the water around the fish. The fish can use this information to tell when something is coming toward it.

Electrosense

Every time you use your muscles, they produce tiny bursts of **electricity**. This is a flow of **energy** that helps power work. Some fish, particularly sharks, can sense electricity. The hammerhead shark has electricity detectors in its head. The duck-billed platypus is a **mammal** that can sense electricity. Detectors in the platypus's rubbery bill help it to find its **prey** in muddy river bottoms.

The duck-billed platypus is found in rivers in Eastern Australia. Detectors in its bill help the platypus find its prey.

bill

Heat-seeking snakes

Some snakes, such as pit vipers, have sensitive heat detectors located in small pits on their heads. The snakes use this sense to track down prey. They **detect** the heat from their prey's body.

The pit viper's heat detectors are located in dark pits. A pit can be seen here just in front of this snake's eye.

Timeline of Prehistoric Adaptations

Scientists study **fossils** of animals that lived millions of years ago. Fossils are remains from past living things, such as bones, that are found in the soil. These remains allow scientists to figure out what sort of lives the animals led. It shows what the animals might have looked like. Fossils also tell scientists when various **adaptations** first appeared.

The dates in the timeline below are not exact. They might change as scientists make new discoveries.

1,000 million years ago (mya) — The first complex (not basic) life-forms possibly appear.

680 mya — The **ancestors** (long-ago relatives) of jellyfish appear.

630 mya — Animals appear that have a definite front and back and top and bottom. This means animals can move in a definite direction. This makes it easier for them to find food.

590 mya — Animals split into two major groups. One will **evolve** (develop over time) into animals with backbones, called **vertebrates**. The other evolve into animals without backbones, called **invertebrates**.

565 mya — Some animals begin to move themselves around, rather than drifting in the ocean.

530 mya — The first vertebrate appears. It may have been a boneless fish. Other early vertebrates may have been similar to eels.

500 mya — Some animals become **adapted** to spending time on land, rather than just in the sea.

460 mya — Fish divide into groups called bony fish (most modern fish) and cartilaginous fish (sharks and rays).

440 mya	The bony fish divide into two group: ray-finned fish (like the fish we have today) and lobe-finned fish.
400 mya	The oldest-known insect is alive.
397 mya	The first four-legged animals develop from the lobe-finned fish. Some will evolve into the animals we know today.
385 mya	The oldest-known tree is alive. Forests began to spread across Earth.
368 mya	The first **amphibian** appears. (Amphibians are cold-blooded. They have smooth skin like present-day frogs. They are also vertebrates.) It is adapted to breathe in and out of water.
310 mya	The ancestors of dinosaurs, modern **reptiles**, and birds appear. There are also reptiles that will evolve into **mammals**.
250 mya	Most life on Earth is wiped out. The survivors include the ancestors of the dinosaurs.
150 mya	The first bird appears.
140 mya	The first flowering plants appear.
70 mya	The first grasses appear.
50 mya	Different kinds of mammals rapidly begin to develop and spread across Earth.
6 mya	The earliest humans develop from apes. Over time, they learn to walk on two legs. They also learn how to use their hands to make and use tools.
200,000 to 400,000 years ago	The first *Homo sapiens* (present-day humans) appear in Africa.

Glossary

adapt when a living thing develops a feature that lets it survive in a particular environment

adaptation feature a living thing develops in order to survive

amphibian cold-blooded, smooth-skinned animal with a backbone, such as a frog. An amphibian usually has gills when it hatches in the water, but it then transforms into an adult with air-breathing lungs.

ancestor relative from long ago

antifreeze substance added to water to prevent it from freezing

behavior way a living thing acts

bird of prey bird that hunts and kills other animals

blubber layer of fat found under the skin of mammals that live in water, such as whales and seals

burrow tunnel dug by an animal that can serve as an underground home

camouflage colorings or markings that help an animal blend into the background

conifer tree with cones and evergreen leaves, like a pine tree

detect notice or pick up on

detector device that picks up on the presence of something, such as a sound or smell

echolocation ability to detect something, based on the time it takes an echo to bounce back from it

electricity flow of energy that helps power muscles, machines, and more

energy ability to do work

environment surroundings in which a living thing is found

evolve develop and change over time

field of vision everything that can be seen at the same time without turning the head or moving the eyes

fitness capability of a living thing to survive and reproduce

focus adjust the eye to light levels in order to create a clear picture

fossil remains of long-ago living things that are found in the soil, such as bones or the imprint of a leaf

glycoprotein substance that some fish produce in their blood to stop ice crystals from forming in their bodies

hibernate sleep deeply through the winter months to save energy

insulation material used to hold in heat

invertebrate animal without a backbone

jet propulsion movement created by sucking in water and then blasting it out again

joint connecting part between bones that allows movement

lateral line sense organs of fish used to detect changes in the water

lens part of the eye that focuses light

mammal warm-blooded animal with a backbone and fur or hair. Female mammals make milk to feed to their young.

migrate move from one area to another every year or season

mimic act or look like another animal

natural selection process by which the living things that are best adapted to their environment become more common than those that are not as well adapted

predator animal that lives by catching and eating other animals

prey animal that is caught and eaten by another animal

reptile cold-blooded animal with a backbone that is often covered with scales, such as a lizard. Reptiles usually lay eggs.

sonar instrument that uses sound waves to detect objects underwater

sound wave traveling sound energy

spine series of bones (called vertebrae) along an animal's back that protect something called the spinal cord

streamlined having a design that lets air or water pass by easily

swim bladder air-filled bag inside some fish. By adjusting the amount of air in the bladder, the fish can move up or down in the water.

talon sharp, hooked claw found on the feet of birds of prey

tendon tough band that connects muscle to bone in the body

venomous able to inject poison into another living thing, through a bite or sting

vertebrate animal with a backbone

Find Out More

Books

Biskup, Agnieszka. *A Journey into Adaptation with Max Axiom, Super Scientist* (Graphic Science). Mankato, Minn.: Capstone, 2007.

Brasch, Nicolas. *Plant and Animal Survival* (The Science Behind). Mankato, Minn.: Smart Apple Media, 2011.

Dell, Pamela. *How Animals Move* (Animal Behavior). Mankato, Minn.: Capstone, 2005.

Gates, Phil. *Nature Got There First.* New York: Kingfisher, 2010.

Parker, Steve. *Adaptation* (Life Processes). Chicago: Heinemann Library, 2006.

Websites

www.kmuska.com/ocean/oceanx.html
Experience an "Ocean Quest": find all about life in a coral reef, including adaptations for living in the ocean.

http://projectbeak.org/adaptations/start.htm
Take a look at some of the many adaptations of birds to their different environments.

http://faculty.washington.edu/chudler/amaze.html
Learn some amazing facts about animal senses.

http://kids.nationalgeographic.com/kids/animals/creaturefeature/
Learn more details about all kinds of amazing animals.

DVDs/Blue-ray

Life, narrated by David Attenborough, BBC/Warner Brothers, 2010

Planet Earth, narrated by David Attenborough, BBC/Warner Brothers, 2007

Topics to research

Alien adaptations

Imagine what shapes life might take on other planets. Think about how conditions on other planets could be different from those on Earth. For example, what sorts of adaptations might life need to survive in the oceans far beneath the icy surface of Jupiter's moon, Europa?

Check out these websites for some ideas:

www.solstation.com/life/eur-life.htm

http://channel.nationalgeographic.com/channel/extraterrestrial/ax/main_fs.html

Marine mammals

Whales and dolphins are air-breathing mammals, just as we are. But they spend all of their lives in the ocean. How have they become adapted to this watery life? Some differences between whales and land mammals are obvious. For example, a whale has flippers instead of legs, to push itself through the water. But what other differences are there? How does a whale stay warm? How does it survive while diving hundreds of feet beneath the surface?

You might find some answers here:

www.thewildclassroom.com/cetaceans/adaptations.html

www.gma.org/marinemammals/adaptations.html

http://seagrant.uaf.edu/marine-ed/mm/fieldguide/adaptations.html

Index